Smithsonian

LITTLE EXPLORER

Sound

by Megan Cooley Peterso

PEBBLE
a capstone imprint

Little Explorer is published by Pebble,
1710 Roe Crest Drive, North Mankato, Minnesota 56003
www.capstonepub.com

Library of Congress Cataloging-in-Publication Data
Names: Peterson, Megan Cooley, author.
Title: Sound / by Megan Cooley Peterson. Description: North Mankato, Minnesota :
Pebble, a Capstone imprint, [2020] | Series: Smithsonian little explorer. Little
physicist | Audience: 6–8. | Audience: K to Grade 3. Identifiers: LCCN 2019004985 |
ISBN 9781977109910 (hardcover) | ISBN 1977109918 (hardcover) | ISBN 9781977110671
(pbk.) | ISBN 1977110673 (pbk.) | ISBN 9781977109927 (eBook PDF) | ISBN 1977109926
(eBook PDF) Subjects: LCSH: Sound—Juvenile literature. Classification:
LCC QC225.5 .P455 2020 | DDC 534--dc23 LC record available at
https://lccn.loc.gov/2019004985

Editorial Credits
Michelle Parkin, editor; Kyle Grenz, designer; Eric Gohl, media researcher;
Tori Abraham, production specialist

Our very special thanks to Henry D. Winter III, PhD, Astrophysicist, Center for
Astrophysics, Harvard and Smithsonian. Capstone would also like to thank
Kealy Gordon, Product Development Manager, and the following at Smithsonian
Enterprises: Ellen Nanney, Licensing Manager; Brigid Ferraro, Vice President, Education
and Consumer Products; and Carol LeBlanc, Senior Vice President, Education and
Consumer Products.

Image Credits
Alamy: Andriy Popov, 8–9; Getty Images: The Washington Post, 27 (inset); iStockphoto:
Elizabeth Hoffmann, 13 (bottom); Newscom: Ingram Publishing, 29; Science Source:
Stephen Dalton, 21; Shutterstock: AJP, 10, Alila Medical Media, 13 (top), Andrey
Armyagov, 8 (inset), blurAZ, 18, Cristi Kerekes, 6 (inset), Eva Kali, 15, Evannovostro,
background (throughout), kiberstalker, 22, Kurdanfell, 9 (water), mareandmare, 6–7,
narikan, 14, Nikita_Stepanov, 26–27, Panaiotidi, 21 (inset), Panptys, 9 (wind), Peter
Porrini, 28, Prathan Nakdontree, 1, PrinceOfLove, cover, Redmich, 17 (top), Roman
Sotola, 9 (steel), Rudmer Zwerver, 17 (bottom), solar22, 11, stockfour, 5, Tomas Kotouc, 4,
trgrowth, 23 (right), Trofimov Denis, 25, Vecton, 19; Wikimedia: Arthur Anker, 23 (left)

All internet sites appearing in back matter were available and accurate when this book
was sent to press.

Printed in the United States of America.
PA70

Table of Contents

What Is Sound?

The world is alive with sound. Birds chirp. The wind blows. Leaves crunch under your feet as you walk. We use sound to talk to each other.

Sound is a type of energy. When particles vibrate, they make sound. Unwrap a piece of candy. Particles in the wrapper bounce against each other. They make a crinkling sound.

Animals also use sound to communicate. Humpback whales sing during mating season. Their songs are made up of clicks, groans, and whistles.

humpback whales

Energy is the ability to do work or make something happen. Heat warms things up. Electricity powers things. Sound energy moves through the air.

Sound Waves

Sound moves in waves. Drop a pebble in a pond. The water spreads out in all directions. Sound waves look similar.

Strong sound waves can move objects. Place a piece of paper on top of a speaker. Next, put some candy sprinkles onto the paper. Now turn on the music. As you turn up the volume, the sprinkles move.

A sound wave is also called a pressure wave. Sound waves move back and forth.

A sound wave loses energy as it moves. Stand next to a friend and say hello. Now go into another room. Say hello again. To your friend, your voice sounds quieter. The sound wave has less energy when it reaches her.

If you tried to yell in outer space, you wouldn't make a sound. There is no air in space for sound waves to move through.

How Sound Waves Move

Press your ear against a wall. Now lightly knock on the wall. You can hear the sound move through the wall. Sound waves can't move by themselves. The waves need something to move through. Sound waves move through liquids, solids, and gases.

How Fast Sound Travels

through air at sea level
1,116 feet (340 meters) per second

through ocean water
4,924 feet (1,500 m) per second

through steel
16,404 feet (5,000 m) per second

Making Sounds

Sing your favorite song. Tell a funny joke. Whisper a secret. You use your voice to do all of these things. But how does your voice work?

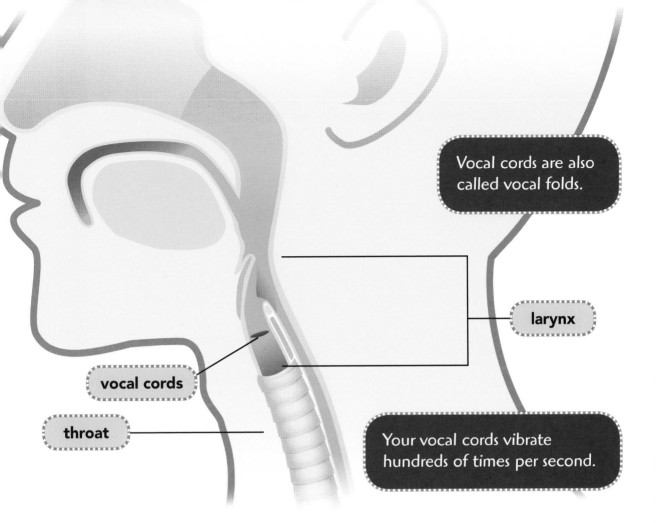

Vocal cords are also called vocal folds.

larynx

vocal cords

throat

Your vocal cords vibrate hundreds of times per second.

Humans have two vocal cords. They are found in the larynx. Vocal cords are thin, stretched-out bands of muscle. When you speak, your lungs blow air against these cords. The cords quickly move back and forth, or vibrate. Vocal cords send sound waves out through your mouth.

Hearing Sounds

Sound waves are always on the move. We use our ears to hear them. Here's how it works. The sound waves hit the outer ear. The ear canal funnels the sound to the eardrum. The eardrum is a piece of tightly stretched skin. The sound waves make the eardrum vibrate. Tiny bones in the inner ear move the vibrations to the cochlea. A nerve inside the cochlea sends sound signals to the brain. The brain identifies the sound.

Having two ears helps your brain figure out a sound's direction.

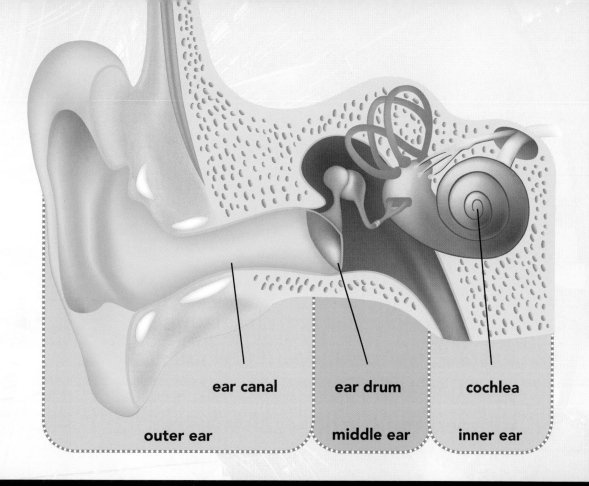

ear canal

ear drum

cochlea

outer ear

middle ear

inner ear

Cochlear Implants

A device called a cochlear implant helps a person with a hearing impairment hear sounds. The device is placed inside the ear. A microphone picks up sounds. These sounds are sent to the cochlea's nerve.

Loud or Soft?

Why are some sounds quiet while others are loud? Stronger vibrations make louder sounds. Place your hand on your throat. Now yell or scream. Do you feel the strong buzzing in your throat? Now put your hand on your throat and whisper. The buzzing feels weaker.

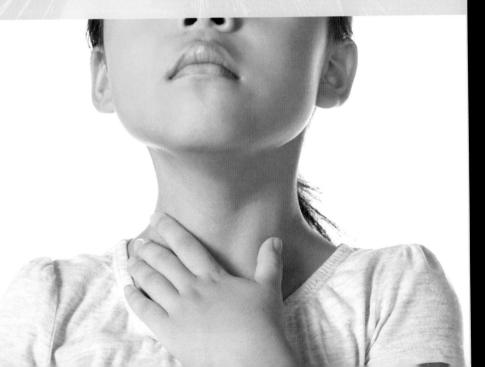

An erupting volcano is the loudest natural sound on Earth.

Loudness is also called amplitude. More amplitude equals a louder sound.

Pitch and Frequency

A lion's roar sounds lower than a mouse's high squeak. The highness or lowness of a sound is called pitch. You can change the pitch of your voice by using your vocal cords.

Sounds vibrate at different speeds. This speed is called frequency. Frequency is how tightly a sound wave is bunched together. A sound wave that is bunched together tightly has a high pitch. A sound wave that is spread out has a low pitch.

Dogs can hear sounds that we can't. That's because dogs hear sounds at higher frequencies than humans.

The Doppler Effect

Imagine that you're outside. A fire truck speeds along the street in front of you. The siren rings out. The sound waves are bunched up in front of the truck. Because the sound waves are bunched together, the siren has a higher pitch.

As the fire truck drives away from you, the siren has a lower pitch. That's because the sound waves stretch out. This is called the Doppler effect.

If you were riding in the fire truck, the siren's pitch would not change.

The Doppler Effect

Austrian scientist Christian Doppler studied sound and light in the 1800s. He noticed that when the source of a sound moved, the sound's pitch changed. The Doppler effect was named after him.

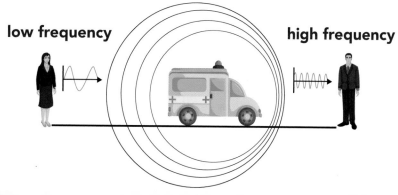

low frequency   high frequency

Echoes

Stand in a small room without a lot of furniture. Now yell. Can you hear the echo? When sound waves hit objects, sometimes they bounce back. This bouncing back is called an echo. Sound bounces off of hard, smooth objects. Wooden floors, concrete buildings, mountains, and caves make sounds bounce. Soft objects, such as carpet or grass, absorb sounds. They don't make echoes.

Some bat species use echoes to find food. It's called echolocation. The bat makes a high-pitched sound. This sound bounces off of bugs nearby. The bat uses its large ears to locate where the bugs are.

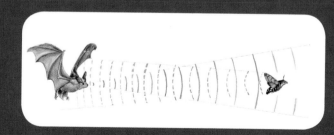

Measuring Sound

Sounds can be measured in different ways. A sound's loudness is measured in decibels. People talk at about 60 decibels. A whisper is 20 decibels. Sounds that are more than 85 decibels can cause hearing damage in humans. Heavy traffic is about 85 decibels. Firecrackers are 150 decibels or higher. Sounds this loud can tear a human eardrum.

The frequency of a sound is measured in hertz. One hertz equals one vibration per second. Humans can hear sounds from 20 to about 20,000 hertz.

A species of shrimp kills its prey with sound. When the Pink Floyd pistol shrimp snaps its large claw, the sound can reach 210 decibels. This kills nearby fish.

Decibel Levels of Common Items

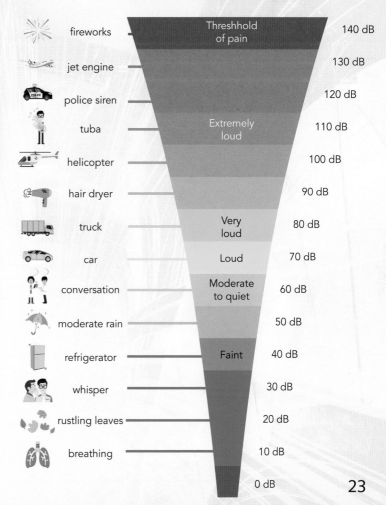

fireworks	Threshhold of pain — 140 dB
jet engine	130 dB
police siren	120 dB
tuba	Extremely loud — 110 dB
helicopter	100 dB
hair dryer	90 dB
truck	Very loud — 80 dB
car	Loud — 70 dB
conversation	Moderate to quiet — 60 dB
moderate rain	50 dB
refrigerator	Faint — 40 dB
whisper	30 dB
rustling leaves	20 dB
breathing	10 dB
	0 dB

Using Sound

Making Music

People use sound to make music. Clap your hands. Sing a song. You're making music by using vibrations. Musical instruments also use vibrations to make sound. Drums have a tight skin that is pulled across the top. When you hit a drum, the skin vibrates. A clarinet has a small piece of wood called a reed. The reed vibrates as you blow air over it.

How an acoustic guitar makes sound.

When a guitar is plucked, the strings vibrate. The strings make sounds. The sounds travel into the guitar's sound hole. The hole makes the sounds louder.

Of all my inventions, I liked the phonograph best . . .

–Thomas Edison

Thomas Edison invented the phonograph in 1877. The device could record and replay sound.

Some studies suggest that listening to music makes people healthier.

Many tools and everyday items use sound. When you listen to music or watch TV, a speaker makes sound. First electricity flows into the speaker. Magnets inside the speaker move back and forth very quickly. They vibrate a paper cone. The cone pushes the sound out of the speaker.

History of Sound

350 BC
Greek philosopher Aristotle says that sound moves through the air.

1500
Leonardo da Vinci discovers that sound travels in waves.

1877
Thomas Edison invents the phonograph.

1927
The first movie featuring the sound of people talking is released.

Two college students invented a fire extinguisher that uses sound to put out fires. The extinguisher makes a low-frequency sound. This removes oxygen in the air. Without oxygen, the fire goes out.

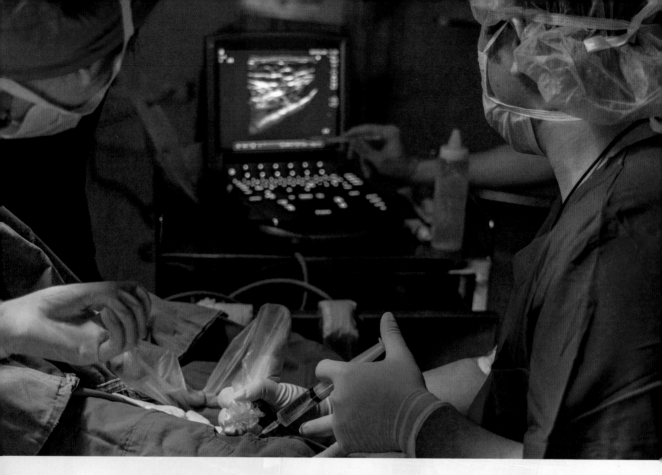

Doctors use echoes to help their patients. An ultrasound machine sends high-frequency sound waves into a patient's body. These waves bounce back to the machine. The machine then makes a picture of the inside of the body. Doctors use these images to decide what might be causing a person's heath problems.

Ships and aircraft use echoes to travel through the sea and air. A machine called sonar sends out sound waves. These waves bounce off objects. The craft uses this information to tell how far away an object is.

Toothed whales use echoes underwater. The whales use their heads to make sounds. These sounds travel through the water and bounce off objects. This tells the whales what to avoid as they swim.

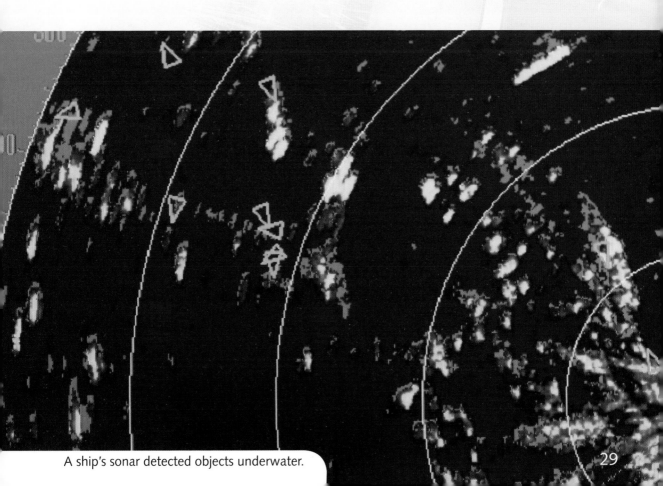

A ship's sonar detected objects underwater.

29

Glossary

amplitude (AM-pluh-tood)—the loudness or softness of a sound

cochlea (KOH-klee-uh)—a spiral-shaped part of the ear that helps send sound messages to the brain

Doppler effect (DAH-pluhr uh-FEKT)—the way wave frequency seems to change depending on how a source of waves, such as a siren, and an observer move toward or away from each other

electricity (i-lek-TRIS-i-tee)—a natural force that can be used to make light and heat or to make machines work

energy (E-nuhr-jee)—the ability to do work, such as moving things or giving heat or light

frequency (FREE-kwuhn-see)—the number of sound waves that pass a location in a certain amount of time

larynx (LAR-ingks)—the upper part of the trachea; the larynx holds the vocal cords

nerve (NURV)—a thin fiber that carries messages between the brain and other parts of the body

particle (PAR-tuh-kuhl)—a tiny piece of something

pitch (PICH)—the highness or lowness of a sound; low pitches have low frequencies and high pitches have high frequencies

sonar (SOH-nar)—a device that uses sound waves to find underwater objects

ultrasound machine (UHL-truh-sound muh-SHEEN)—a medical device that takes images inside the body

vibration (vye-BRAY-shuhn)—a fast movement back and forth

Critical Thinking Questions

1. How is a sound wave made? Which direction do sound waves travel?

2. Do sounds travel faster through the air or through water? Why?

3. Why is a scream louder than a whisper?

Read More

James, Emily. *The Simple Science of Sound.* Simply Science. North Mankato, MN: Capstone Press, 2018.

Johnson, Robin. *What Are Sound Waves?* Light and Sound Waves Close-Up. St. Catherines, Ontario; New York: Crabtree Publishing Company, 2014.

Pfeffer, Wendy. *Sounds All Around.* Let's-Read-and-Find-Out Science. New York: Harper, 2016.

Internet Sites

DK Find Out. Sound.
https://www.dkfindout.com/us/science/sound/

The Science of Sound.
https://kids.nationalgeographic.com/explore/youtube-playlist-pages/youtube-playlist-sound/

Index